Dirty Words
of Wisdom

Library of Congress Cataloging in Publication Number: 2003090704

ISBN: 1-931686-64-5

Printed in Singapore

Typeset in Bodoni, Futura, Linoscript, Poetica, Zaph Dingbats

Designed by Bryn Ashburn

Cross-stitch on the cover and page 3 by Erin Slonaker

Cross-stitch on the cover and page 3 photographed by William Drake

Interior photos, pages 1, 10, 18–19, 21, 22–23, 26–27, 30–31, 34–35, 38–39, 42–43, 46–47, 51, 52–53, 58, 64–65, 70–71, 76–77, 78–79, 84–85, 86, 90–91, 95 courtesy of Getty Images

Interior photos, pages 74, 96 courtesy of Art Today

Interior photo, pages 14–15 courtesy of NASA

Distributed in North America by Chronicle Books
85 Second Street
San Francisco, CA 94105

10 9 8 7 6 5 4 3 2 1

Quirk Books
215 Church Street
Philadelphia, PA 19106
www.quirkbooks.com

DIRTY WORDS of WISDOM

A TREASURY OF CLASSIC ?✳✳@! QUOTATIONS

Edited by
Sam Stall & Lou Harry

QUIRK·BOOKS
· PHILADELPHIA ·

Gentle Reader,

You hold in your hands a work centuries in the making—a survey of pungent quotes uttered by politicians, writers, movie stars, and other luminaries great and small.

Some are witty.

Some are observant.

All endeavor, either by accident or by design, to teach us something—even if it's only that the person who uttered them had a screw loose.

Their subject matter covers the gamut. The only thing they have in common is that each includes at least one "dirty" word.

Does the world need more swearing? No. Not at a time when even sixth-graders spew out the sorts of X-rated tirades once reserved for Marine Corps drill instructors and Hollywood studio moguls.

What the world needs is *better* swearing. And that's what this book is all about. Today, when curses are as omnipresent in conversation as Muzak is on elevators, it's helpful to hear them used by people who consider four-letter words to be the verbal versions of nuclear missiles. Like nukes, it's best to keep them in reserve, deploying them only when you need to make a big, big impression.

Instead of pocking every other sentence with one of George Carlin's famed seven words you can't say on television, many of the big names listed in this book use bad words sparingly. Their example proves that, in the hands of a competent practitioner, curses can cut through the clatter of everyday conversation, making a point clearly. Done properly, this technique approaches art.

Of course, our gang of potty-mouthed pundits also includes All the Usual Suspects—everyone from Ozzy Osbourne to Chris Rock. However, it also contains plenty of people who didn't make a living being obscene. Many of their utterances wouldn't even be considered dirty by today's crass standards. Are "damn," "hell," and "whore" even swear words anymore?

Nevertheless, they made our list, in part because they come from a time when even the mildest expletive could quiet a room faster than a judge's gavel. Plus it's fun to hear some of these prim nineteenth-century ladies and gentlemen get down and dirty. So I guess you could say we graded on a sliding scale. Madonna using the F word 15 times in one sentence just isn't as interesting as Edna St. Vincent Millay saying "damn."

Finally, a warning to literary pedants. If you find that our version of a famous quote doesn't quite jibe with the

one you've seen or heard, don't worry about it. Some of
our luminaries used their signature lines over and over,
changing them slightly each time. General George S.
Patton, for instance, seems to have shared his bit about
"letting the other sonofabitch die for his country" with
everybody. He probably whispered it to his kids at bed-
time. In a similar vein, even if evidence suggests that
some of our luminaries didn't speak quite as succinctly as
history says they did, we chose to go with posterity's second (and usually much more pithy) draft. We think if our
subjects were still around, they'd concur.

If nothing else, these quotes prove that the judicious
use of profanity enlivens conversation the way hot sauce
enlivens a meal. Use too much and you make an unpalat-
able mess; use just a little and you give everything a
spicy edge.

Open-minded aficionados of colorful language, read
and enjoy. All others are cordially invited to kiss our
asses.

❧ Sam Stall & Lou Harry

If at first you don't succeed, try again. Then quit. No use being a damn fool about it.

—W. C. Fields, comedian

Do what you feel in your
heart to be right—for you'll
be criticized anyway.
You'll be damned if you do
and damned if you don't.

—Eleanor Roosevelt, first lady

THE TRUTH WILL SET YOU FREE.

BUT FIRST, IT WILL PISS YOU OFF.

—GLORIA STEINEM, FEMINIST

THE HELL WITH THE HAIR ON YOUR HEAD. IT'S THE HAIR ON YOUR CHEST THAT COUNTS.

—HUMPHREY BOGART, ACTOR

I think it's inevitable
that you go through the
hard fucked-up stuff. If
you're alive on this earth,
it's going to happen, so
I'm not worried.

—ALANIS MORISSETTE, MUSICIAN

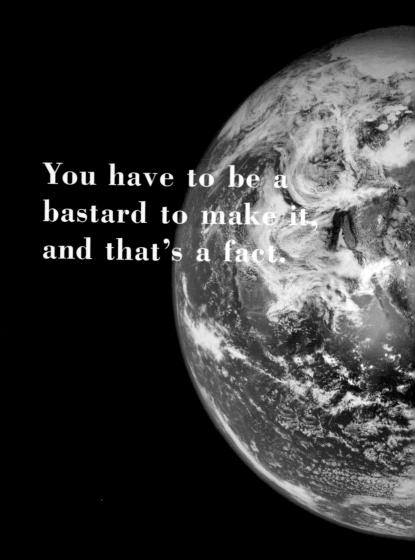

You have to be a
bastard to make it,
and that's a fact.

And the Beatles are the biggest bastards on earth.

—John Lennon, musician

My dad always used
to tell me that if they
challenge you to an after-
school fight, tell them
you won't wait —you can
kick their ass right now.

—Cameron Diaz, actress

I always followed my father's advice: He told me to never insult anybody unintentionally. So if I insult you, you can be goddamn sure I intend to.

—John Wayne, actor

My childhood was a period of waiting for the moment when I could send everyone and everything connected with it to hell.

—IGOR STRAVINSKY, COMPOSER

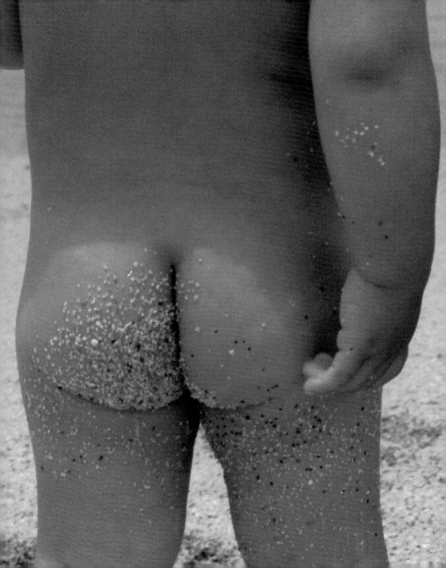

AS A CHILD,
IF SOMEONE TELLS
YOU YOU'RE FUCKING
WORTHLESS, YOU
BECOME FUCKING
WORTHLESS.

—OZZY OSBOURNE, MUSICIAN

My mother
never saw the irony
in calling me a
son of a bitch.

—JACK NICHOLSON, ACTOR

I want to do everything for my kid. Work with him. Raise him. Nourish him. Spend time with him. And sixteen years from now, he's going to do to me what I did to my father. He's going to walk right up to me, look me right in the eye, and go, "God, Dad, you're fucked."

—ROBIN WILLIAMS, ACTOR

Every man is a damn fool
for at least five minutes every
day; wisdom consists of not
exceeding that limit.

—Elbert Hubbard, author

I've made an ass of myself
so many times I often wonder
if I am one.

—Norman Mailer, author

ONCE YOU HAVE YELLED AND
SCREAMED AT YOUR FRIEND ON
AN UNIMPORTANT MATTER OR
EVEN AN IMPORTANT MATTER,
YOU MUST ADMIT THAT YOU
ARE A FUCKING IDIOT AND
APOLOGIZE IMMEDIATELY.

—WILLIE NELSON, MUSICIAN

Guilt

is the pruning shears that society
developed to prevent you from growing
into an even bigger asshole than
you already are.

—Dennis Miller, comedian

WHEN I DIE,
I HOPE TO GO
TO HEAVEN,

WHATEVER THE
HELL THAT IS.

—AYN RAND, AUTHOR

I once asked a Jesuit priest what was the best short prayer he knew. He said, "Fuck it," as in, "Fuck it, it's in God's hands."

—Anthony Hopkins, actor

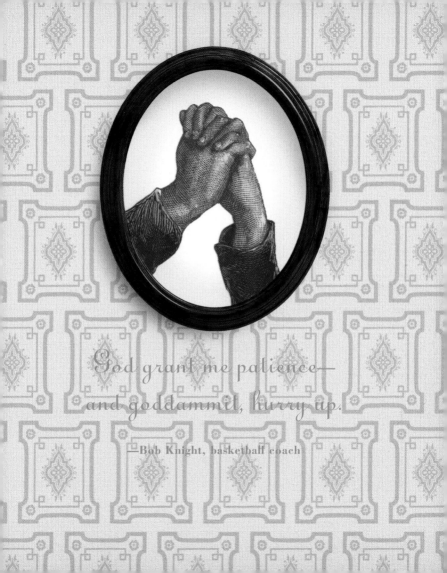

God grant me patience—
and goddammit, hurry up.

—Bob Knight, basketball coach

The road to
Hell is

paved with good
intentions.

—Samuel Johnson, scholar

I DON'T BELIEVE
IN SHIT, UNTIL
SHIT HAPPENS.

—Bernie Mac, comedian

I have my own God, and I think
my God finds me incredibly fucking
funny. That's why I chose
him as my God.

—Dennis Miller, comedian

DON'T BE A FOOL
AND DIE FOR YOUR
COUNTRY. ✷✷✷

LET THE OTHER SON OF
A BITCH DIE FOR HIS. ✭ ✭

—GENERAL GEORGE S. PATTON

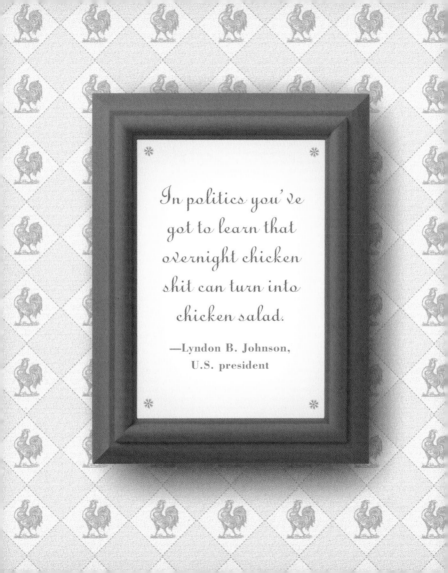

In politics you've got to learn that overnight chicken shit can turn into chicken salad.

—Lyndon B. Johnson, U.S. president

Take away the right to
say "fuck," and you take
away the right to say,
"Fuck the government."

✶ ✶ ✶ ✶ ✶ ✶

—Lenny Bruce, comedian

Politics is just like show business. You have a hell of an opening, coast for a while, and then have a hell of a close.

—Ronald Reagan, U.S. president

I ALWAYS FIGURED THE AMERICAN PEOPLE WANTED A SOLEMN ASS FOR PRESIDENT, SO I WENT ALONG WITH THEM.

—CALVIN COOLIDGE, U.S. PRESIDENT

He may be a son
of a bitch, but he's our
son of a bitch.

—Franklin D. Roosevelt, U.S. president

The principal difference between the husbandry-man and the historian is that the former breeds sheep or cows or such, and the latter breeds (assumed) facts. The husbandryman uses his skills to enrich the future; the historian uses his to enrich the past. Both are usually up to their ankles in bullshit.

—TOM ROBBINS, AUTHOR

WHEN A MAN
GIVES HIS OPINION
HE'S A MAN. WHEN
A WOMAN GIVES
HER OPINION
SHE'S A BITCH.

—BETTE DAVIS, ACTRESS

"BITCH" MEANS
A WOMAN WHO
WILL GO TO BED
WITH EVERYONE
BUT YOU.

—CYNTHIA HEIMEL, AUTHOR

People say to me,
"You're not very feminine."
Well, they can suck
my dick.

—ROSEANNE, ACTRESS

I'm as confident as Cleopatra's pussy.

—BETTE MIDLER, ACTRESS AND SINGER

Beauty, to me, is
about being comfortable
in your own skin.

That, or a kick-ass
red lipstick.

— GWYNETH PALTROW, ACTRESS

I like having a good pair
of tits on me and a good ass.
If I didn't, I don't think
I'd feel attractive.

—KATE WINSLET, ACTRESS

I GET SO UGLY WHEN I
FUCK. AND I DON'T CARE. AND
IF YOU CARE ABOUT WHAT
I LOOK LIKE WHEN YOU'RE
FUCKING ME, YOU SHOULDN'T
BE FUCKING ME IN THE
FIRST PLACE.

—MARGARET CHO, COMEDIAN

Rock is really about dick and testosterone. I go see a band, I wanna fuck the guy—that's the way it is; it's always been that way.

—COURTNEY LOVE, MUSICIAN

MY FIRST REACTION TO PORNO
FILMS IS AS FOLLOWS: AFTER
THE FIRST TEN MINUTES I WANT
TO GO HOME AND SCREW. AFTER
THE FIRST TWENTY MINUTES, I
NEVER WANT TO SCREW AGAIN
AS LONG AS I LIVE.

—ERICA JONG, AUTHOR

A woman knows if she's gonna fuck you in the first five minutes of meeting you. Women know right away. Women know on the handshake. As they grip your hand, if they like you, they're thinking, "I'm gonna fuck him. I hope he don't say nothing too stupid."

—Chris Rock, comedian

I FIND SUGGESTION A HELL
OF A LOT MORE PROVOCATIVE THAN
EXPLICIT DETAIL. YOU DIDN'T SEE
CLARK [GABLE] AND VIVIEN [LEIGH]
ROLLING AROUND IN BED IN
GONE WITH THE WIND, BUT YOU
SAW THAT SHIT-EATING GRIN ON HER
FACE THE NEXT MORNING AND YOU
KNEW DAMNED WELL SHE'D
GOTTEN PROPERLY LAID.

—JOAN CRAWFORD, ACTRESS

We're not supposed
to mention fucking in mixed
company, but that's exactly
where it takes place.

—GEORGE CARLIN, COMEDIAN

You can't talk about fucking
in America. People say you're
dirty. But if you talk about killing
somebody, that's cool.

—RICHARD PRYOR, COMEDIAN

Sex is interesting, but it's not totally important. . . . A man can go seventy years without a piece of ass, but he can die in a week without a bowel movement.

—CHARLES BUKOWSKI, AUTHOR

You're young,
you're drunk, you're
in bed, you have knives;
shit happens.

—Angelina Jolie, actress

You can prick
your finger but don't
finger your prick.

—GEORGE CARLIN, COMEDIAN

I don't mind bad words—for instance, fuck. I think it's amazing that it's a swear word. After all, it's something most everyone likes doing. It's sweet and harmless. We've overanalyzed things to make something pejorative out of an experience that's so nice.

—Rupert Everett, actor

I don't give a damn for a man who can only spell a word one way.

—Mark Twain, author

The most essential gift for a good writer is a built-in, shockproof, shit detector.

—Ernest Hemingway, author

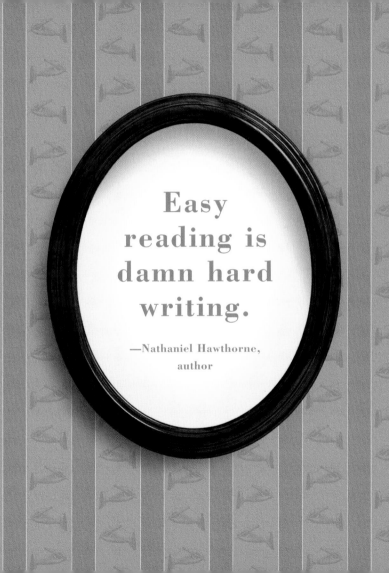

Easy
reading is
damn hard
writing.

—Nathaniel Hawthorne,
author

I'm so sick of this "ain't humanity great" bullshit. We're a virus in shoes, people. That's all we are.

—BILL HICKS, COMEDIAN

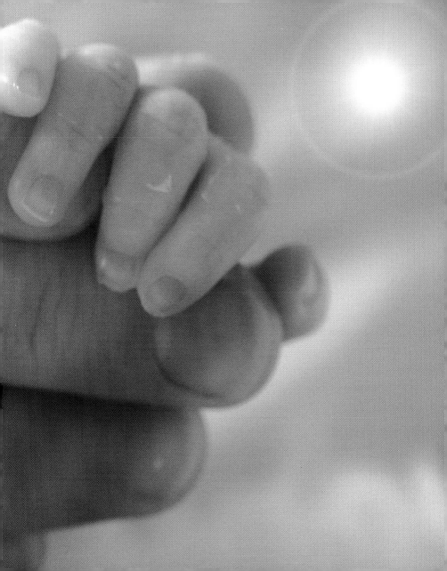

I tell you, we are here on
Earth to fart around, and don't let
anybody tell you different.

—Kurt Vonnegut, author

If you wind up with a boring, miserable life because you listened to your mom, your dad, your teacher, your priest, or some guy on television telling you how to do your shit, then you deserve it.

—Frank Zappa, musician

Not only is life a bitch, it has puppies.

—ADRIENNE E. GUSOFF, AUTHOR

It's not true that life is one
damn thing after another—it's one
damn thing over and over.

—EDNA ST. VINCENT MILLAY, POET

IN LIFE THERE
ARE NO WINNERS,

ONLY ASSHOLES
WITH SWISS BANK
ACCOUNTS.

—MATTHEW LOTTI, AUTHOR

The snow doesn't give a soft

white damn whom it touches.

—E. E. CUMMINGS, POET

I've always known that the whole society line was bullshit from wall to wall, but what society does is cover the bullshit with chocolate so you think it's bridge mix.

—FLORYNCE KENNEDY, FEMINIST

MAKE THE CUSTOMER THINK HE'S GETTING LAID WHEN HE'S GETTING FUCKED.

—Michael Bloomberg, businessman and mayor of New York City

WHEN SHIT BECOMES VALUABLE, THE POOR WILL BE BORN WITHOUT ASSHOLES.

—HENRY MILLER, AUTHOR

I'm not a paranoid deranged millionaire. Goddammit, I'm a billionaire!

—Howard Hughes, billionaire

THE SUN DON'T SHINE ON THE SAME DOG'S ASS ALL THE TIME.

—CATFISH HUNTER, BASEBALL PLAYER

You can lead a whore
to culture

but you can't make

her think. 🌸

—Dorothy Parker, author

You've got to love livin', baby,
because dyin' is a pain in the ass!

—Frank Sinatra, musician

IF ALL ELSE FAILS, GO FOR THE DICK JOKE.

—ROBIN WILLIAMS, ACTOR

I DRANK TO DROWN MY SORROWS,

BUT NOW THE DAMNED THINGS
HAVE LEARNED TO SWIM.

—FRIDA KAHLO, ARTIST

THE DEADLIEST BULLSHIT IS ODORLESS AND TRANSPARENT.

—William Gibson, author